Workplace Communication Styles

A tested and trusted guide to a sustainable workplace relationship for a healthy interpersonal interactivity and increased productivity.

Henry Mark

Copyright © 2021 Henry Mark

All rights reserved. No part of this publication may be reproduced, distributed, or transmitted in any form or by any means including photocopying, recording or other mechanical or electronic methods without the prior written permission of the publisher or from copyright holder, except in the case of brief quotations embodied in critical reviews and certain other non-commercial uses permitted by copyright law.

Disclaimer

This book is designed to provide information about the subject matter covered. It was sold with an understanding that the publisher and author were not rendering professional services of any kind. If expert assistance is required, then it should be sought first and foremost from a competent professional who can offer you appropriate guidance on your particular needs before considering anything else contained within the pages of this guide. Every effort has been made to make this book as complete and accurate as possible. However, there may still exist mistakes both in typography (spelling) errors and also content-wise which will hopefully be corrected by future editions if necessary.

The stories outlined within this book, while based in part on fact, have been modified so as not to reveal the identity of any real person. Any resemblance between people depicted in this book either living or dead persons is strictly coincidental. The purpose of this book is to enlighten, inspire, and entertain the reader. Neither author nor publisher shall be liable for damages caused directly or indirectly by information presented herein.

Table of Contents

INTRODUCTION 5
CHAPTER ONE 9
   WHAT ARE COMMUNICATION STYLES? 9
CHAPTER TWO 21
   GET TO KNOW YOUR PREDOMINANT COMMUNICATION STYLE 21
CHAPTER THREE 33
   TIPS FOR MORE EFFECTIVE COMMUNICATION 33
CHAPTER FOUR 41
   THE IMPORTANCE OF UNDERSTANDING COMMUNICATION STYLES . 41
CHAPTER FIVE 47
     CONCLUSION 47

INTRODUCTION

Communication is an essential and inherent aspect of human existence. It is the main tool used by human beings to express needs and feelings. It occurs when we transmit a message and receive a response. But there are different styles of interpersonal communication and we often need to manage them all in the same company. A style of communication is the set of expressive qualities that are characteristic of the sender of a message. We spend a large part of our time communicating and everything we do, every gesture, every look, is a form of communication. The complexity of human relationships and the fact that communicating is already an automatic act makes it not always easy for us to adopt effective communication.

Each of us has our own communication style that may vary depending on circumstances. Our communication style is not always the most effective, but it is possible for us to shape the way we communicate. During interpersonal interaction, one must be able to identify and understand the communication style of the other. This is important in order to maintain a healthy relationship with your colleagues in the workplace as well as others you come across such as relatives, friends or acquaintances.

The importance of identifying different styles can be seen when we consider what happens when people are unaware that their conversational counterpart has a different style from them: they often experience difficulty interacting effectively. This inability to interact effectively may result in adverse consequences for both parties, such as acute stress reaction (e.g., anxiety), miscommunication, misunderstanding and impaired professional performance. Thus, if an individual is not able to identify his communication counterpart's style and adjust within the setting, he or she may find him-or herself in a realm of distress with feelings of anxiety. It is of the essence to understand that there are different ways an individual may communicate with another. This is because people have their own perception and frame of reference when they receive communication input in a particular situation. The style in which an individual sends his message can be either one of the following: verbal, nonverbal or both.

Additionally, factors such as personality, culture and social status may also influence how one communicates with others.

In this guide, I have explored different communication styles, their advantages and disadvantages and how to develop a more effective communication style that will help you to keep a sustainable relationship with people, especially coworkers for a healthy interpersonal interactivity and increased productivity.

CHAPTER ONE

WHAT ARE COMMUNICATION STYLES?

Communication styles can be defined as the way a person communicates with others. Although people use different methods to express themselves, they should be able to do so in a clear and effective manner when interacting with their colleagues.

A communication style that is appropriate for one scenario may not work well in another. Understanding how to adapt your style helps you get your point across and improves interpersonal relationships within the workplace. Effective communication leads to an increase in productivity, while ineffective communication causes frustration among staff members and managers alike.

Our personality, behavior and the way we think and interact make us adopt different communication styles. We all have a more or less stable way of communicating. We tend to adopt a certain style of communication, which doesn't mean that we always communicate in the same way, but each one of us has a style that ends up being predominant.

The way we communicate is, in a simple way, the way we express ourselves, how we express our feelings and our needs and how we convey a message to others. We can adopt different styles of communication, through: how we defend our perspective and opinion; the way in which we are able to clearly convey our message; the way we consider and respect the other's position; our ability to collaborate with each other; our ability to listen and understand.

We all know how important it is to make our points clearly, but all people communicate differently depending on their background and upbringing. People from different regions have distinct speech patterns and there is a big cultural influence on the way one communicates. However, understanding your own and others' communication style is vital to good interpersonal relationships in the workplace.

What communication styles are there?

We can identify four main distinct styles of communication, constituted by a set of distinguishing characteristics.

1. Aggressive communication style

An aggressive communication style consists of saying everything we think without taking into account the other's opinion. This style of communication is characterized by a focus on one's own goals and devaluation of the other's interests.

Our needs and desires overlap with those of others, with no room for negotiation and little flexibility. By adopting an aggressive communication style, we express our needs or opinions in a demanding and even hostile way.

When we adopt an aggressive communication style, we intend to impose our point of view and dominate. This style of communication may be necessary in some circumstances, for example when we are in a leadership position and intend to enforce our order or directive. However, most of the time it ends up being inappropriate and ineffective, as it tends to generate passive reactions or, on the contrary, frustration and aggressiveness. Aggressive communicators try to dominate the other, they don't give space for a collaboration and a mutual interaction process to exist. Some examples of phrases that fall within the aggressive communication style might be "I'm the boss here", "things have to be done this way", "you're absolutely right in what you're saying".

Aggressive responses include talking loudly, interrupting the other or asking questions before he has finished answering, using the "I" too much, bragging, expressing opinions as if they were facts, accusing or blaming the other.

Often an aggressive communication style is based on beliefs of superiority (e.g., "I'm better, I know how to do it) but also fear and insecurity (e.g., "nobody can be trusted", "he/she will do have poorly done", "I can't count on others").

Aggressive responses are often reinforced and perpetuated because the person reduces the tension felt and sometimes actually gets what he wants. That is, when you get what you wanted, positive feelings are generated that contribute to maintaining this style of communication. However, in the long run this is a communication style that has negative consequences for interpersonal relationships. People who use this style of communication predominantly tend to blame others for situations and develop warning mechanisms, waiting for possible attacks from others.

People who use an aggressive communication style end up being seen by others as coercive, hostile, intransigent and with difficulties in self-control. Although people may initially give in out of fear, in the long run they will either avoid these people or respond in an aggressive tone as well. So, in the long run, interpersonal relationships deteriorate.

2. Passive communication

Communicating passively is characterized by the expression of feelings, thoughts or opinions in an indirect or implicit way, or even by the total absence of expression.

People with this style often have difficulty expressing their needs and fighting for what they believe. Still, they hesitate to be protagonists in an undertaking, precisely because they want to avoid conflicts and any indisposition.

A passive communication style is characterized by letting the other dominate the communication. There is a tendency not to reveal what we actually think and to say what others want to hear or simply not saying anything and not asserting our point of view. In short, in this style of communication we do not openly assert ourselves and do not speak out, which means that our opinions, desires or thoughts are not communicated.

We often adopt a passive communication style to avoid conflict, to defend ourselves or to run away from certain situations. It is in this style of communication that the difficulty of saying NO is often found. Some phrases that can be inserted in this style of communication are "it's not worth it, nothing is gained from this", "okay, we do it as you want", "it doesn't matter what I think".

Passive responses can include hesitations, avoiding certain subjects, expressing anxiety, long and disconnected sentences, over-justifying, frequent or excessive apologies, expressions of self-deprecation, and expressions that show an annulment of one's needs. Usually, the goal is to please others and avoid conflict and discord at all costs.

The fact that we adopt a passive communication style may have to do with fear of the negative consequences of expressing our opinion, with the perception that the situation is threatening or difficult, with low self-esteem, with confusing good manners. There are usually irrational beliefs of self-devaluation.

When a person adopts a passive communication, he can, initially, reduce the anxiety felt once he managed to avoid the conflict. However, you may also feel guilty or anger at the outcome of the situation, that is, for not being able to assert your position or express what you really thought. Feelings of self-pity can also arise because the person realizes that he has allowed the other person to take advantage of the situation.

In the long run, this difficulty in clearly expressing what one thinks and feels leads people to feelings of devaluation and low self-esteem or even excessive anxiety in situations where they have to interact with others. They end up being seen by others as vulnerable or easily manipulated, often becoming easy targets.

3. Manipulative communication

In the manipulative communication style, the person uses different speeches depending on the people he is addressing. There is no direct and clear involvement in interactions, the person does not say clearly what he wants but uses artifices to obtain it. There is a use of the other to achieve ends or objectives, without however letting it show.

Often in debates, the manipulative communication style manifests itself in someone who does not speak, speaks quietly and in secret, always thinking that "the other does this so that I believe in that". In the long run, this style of communication tends to make us lose credibility, as it prevents us from creating relationships based on mutual trust.

In short, the central feature of this style of communication is the existence of a tactical rather than a genuine relationship with others. I In the manipulative communication style, communication is a means to an end and does not occur collaboratively. The person with a manipulative communication style tends to be critical, both with themselves and with others, presenting a clear difficulty in accepting their mistakes and responsibilities.

Some phrases that can be inserted in the manipulative style are "far from me such an idea", "I only tell you this". It can take the form of sarcasm, blackmail or insinuation.

4. Assertive communication

The assertive communication style or assertive communication is characterized by showing through words and gestures what we really want, think or feel, while encouraging the other to show it too. Assertive communication is a form of communication that is characterized by autonomy and taking responsibility for interactions and relationships. This style of communication encourages honest, open and cooperative forms of communication in relationships.

When we are assertive, we are able to assert our position without disrespecting or invalidating the other's position; we are able to negotiate a conflict and solve problems cooperatively. It is a style of communication that allows us to be truer to ourselves and to others, stating situations clearly, defending our rights without violating those of others.

Assertive communication involves the ability to say "no" without feeling bad about it, since we have our priorities well established and are able to affirm them, also listening to the other side and asking the other to explain what we do not understand. Basically, being assertive implies understanding that others may have a different perspective than ours and one does not have to cancel the other.

Assertive communication is the form of communication that, globally, is most effective, since it generates a climate of trust and openness, where everyone can communicate their points of view.

Assertive answers include writing open-ended questions aimed at knowing the wishes and opinions of others, listening to the other, direct expression of thoughts and feelings, short and direct sentences, ability to distinguish facts from opinions, suggestions and constructive criticisms instead of blame or personal attack.

By adopting an assertive communication style, we are aware of our own rights but also the rights and responsibilities of others. There is a positive relationship between assertiveness and self-esteem, that is, people who are more assertive have better self-esteem. At the base of assertive communication are beliefs centered on accountability and control (eg "I can learn from my mistakes", "I can choose how to communicate with others"). In addition to self-esteem, assertive people also have a greater ability to control their lives and, consequently, greater satisfaction in their relationships and in achieving their goals.

CHAPTER TWO

GET TO KNOW YOUR PREDOMINANT COMMUNICATION STYLE

Communication styles are a predominant trend; however, this does not mean that we always adopt the same style. There is obviously variation depending on specific circumstances and situations. It is rare for someone to be always assertive, or always aggressive. It is easier, for example, to be assertive in situations where we are comfortable, such as communicating with friends, than in situations where we are not so comfortable and have more to lose, such as communicating with a hierarchical superior. We may also be more likely to be aggressive in situations we are used to dominating than in new, unfamiliar situations where we may be slightly more passive.

Thus, communication styles are neither rigid nor watertight and we do not adopt just one. Still, we are generally more likely to communicate in a certain way.

Here, I present some characteristics to understand your predominant style of communication:

Aggressive communication style:
- I am, for the most part, authoritarian and decisive;
- They often criticize me for being always against;
- I have difficulty listening to others;
- I interrupt and cut others off, sometimes without realizing it;
- I feel that intimidating others can be a necessary means of achieving goals;
- When I feel cheated, I get revenge;
- I tend to talk more than others and have difficulty controlling the amount of time I'm talking;
- Sometimes I shock people with my attitudes;

- To make sure things are done right it's better to do them myself;
- I'd rather be "wolf" than "lamb".

Passive communication style:

- I often say "yes", when deep down I want to say "no";
- When there is debate, I prefer to stay in my corner and "see what happens";
- I do everything I can to be discreet and go unnoticed;
- I'd rather never ask a colleague for help; he may think I'm not competent;
- I'm shy and have big blocks when I have to do something unusual;
- I tend to put off the things I have to do later;
- I often leave a job halfway through without finishing it;
- I do my best not to disturb others;
- I have difficulty making decisions;

- I don't like being the only person in a group to think a certain way;
- I know that sometimes I let myself explore a little bit;
- I prefer to observe than participate;
- I'd rather be in the back than in the front row.

Manipulative communication style:

- When I don't know a person well, I prefer to hide what I think or feel;
- It's usually easier for me to act through someone else than directly;
- They consider me, in general, "sly" and skilled in relationships with others;
- I make "tapes" to get what I want;
- I take advantage of things or others and I think that's part of being out of the loop;
- Creating conflicts can be more effective than reducing tensions;
- I'm good at convincing people and imposing my ideas on them;

- I use irony to my advantage;
- Praise, even if it's not sincere, is a good way to get what we want;
- I believe that manipulating others is often the only practical way to get what we want.

Assertive communication style:

- I defend my rights without violating the rights of others;
- I'm not afraid to criticize others and tell them what I think;
- I'm not afraid to refuse certain tasks that are not part of my duties;
- I am not afraid to express my opinion, even to the most hostile people;
- I maintain relationships with others more based on trust than on domination or calculation;
- I am comfortable in face-to-face interactions;
- I am ambitious and I try to achieve my goals;

- In general, I know what I must do to be successful;
- In case of disagreement, I try to reach a meeting point based on the interests of both parties;
- I prefer to expose matters clearly and openly;
- I am generally genuine and show what I am without dissimulation;
- When I don't agree I can say it clearly;
- I'm not afraid to speak in public;
- I think openness is the best way to build trust in relationships with others;
- I know how to listen and I don't cut the word to others;
- I can usually carry through with what I've decided to do;
- I'm not afraid to express my feelings as I feel them;
- I know how to protest effectively and without being too aggressive.

How to shape our communication style more effectively?

Recognizing our style of communication, it is possible to shape the way we communicate and seek to communicate in a more effective way that allows us not only to achieve goals but also to improve our interpersonal relationships, both personally and professionally.

Thus, some strategies can be useful to achieve this:

1. Being able to read the situation and the other person, understanding their position and what they are looking for, as well as their fears and needs.

2. Adjusting our communication to the context we are in and circumstances. For example, we should not adopt the same way of communicating at a job interview and at an informal meeting.

3. We learn to recognize our emotions and develop strategies to effectively manage our emotional states.

4. Being aware of our needs and our qualities, valuing what we are and not being afraid to express it to others.

5. Understand that saying "no" to others is often a way of saying "yes" to ourselves, that is, of respecting our needs.

6. Realize that if we have to demean or annul ourselves in a certain relationship, it's because that relationship isn't worth it.

7. Gaining awareness of our non-verbal communication (gestures, body posture...). We can, for example, practice an oral presentation in front of the mirror or record ourselves performing.

8. Understand that the "no" is always guaranteed and, therefore, if we want something, it is always better to ask for it.

9. Understand that we cannot control another person's behavior but we can take responsibility for our communication and how we communicate. Even if the other person may not have the best posture, we can have it.

10. Accepting challenges and contacting new contexts and different people, as this will give us an important learning experience in terms of communication and trust.

Dealing with different communication styles?

It is important not only to shape our own communication style, but also to learn to deal with people who have different communication styles compared to ours. Below, we share some strategies that you can use with each of the communication styles:

Aggressive communication style

Since the person with an aggressive style has difficulties in respecting the limits, it is important that these are defined very clearly. Set the limits and the importance of having respect right from the start. If the person constantly interrupts, ask them to wait to speak and demonstrate that if there is no opportunity for everyone to speak, they will not reach a consensus. Explain to the person why it is harmful to try to impose your opinion and show that an agreement can be reached. If possible, create opportunities for the person to express their frustration in a more appropriate and less harmful way.

Passive communication style

Try to speak to the person in private as it can be embarrassing for them to speak in front of many people. Encourage him to say what he thinks and show that there is openness and acceptance to do so. Give the person options so that they don't feel too pressured, and express your own opinion or feelings by showing that the person can do it too. Try to start by broaching something the person is most comfortable with. If at any point the person has not expressed much, tell them that they can come to you later if you want to go deeper into the subject.

Manipulative communication style

When communicating with a person with a manipulative communication style it is important to remain calm in conflict situations. It is possible that the person will try to provoke others and get them to express something that they themselves do not have the courage to express. If you notice that the person is unloading on the wrong person, try to direct them, indicating, for example, who they should talk to about this subject. Encourage him to resolve the conflict in a transparent way, and if he fights back, do so gently. Be direct in communication and demonstrate to the person that they can also be direct and that this will bring them more benefits.

Assertive communication style

When communicating with an assertive person, value their communication skills and support their ideas and opinions. Also adopt an assertive style establishing cooperative communication based on trust. Create conditions to listen to the other and so that he can hear you too and try to validate and recognize your point of view, giving them space to communicate.

In short, we all have a distinct communication style and we can shape communication according to circumstances, and it is also possible for us to develop a more effective and collaborative communication.

CHAPTER THREE

TIPS FOR MORE EFFECTIVE COMMUNICATION

Developing good team communication can increase productivity and decrease conflict.

For communication to be efficient it is necessary:

Learn to listen. Understanding the needs behind a speech is very important. A good way to develop this ability is through non-violent communication, which makes us listen to people empathically.

When we are in a dialogue it is important to understand the pain of the other, ask questions that lead people to be more specific and show interest in what they are talking about.

So, whether as a leader or a member of a team, you will be able to gather important information for problem solving.

Be clear and objective. In a leadership position it is critical that you are clear when communicating. Really show all the strategic points behind a project, emphasize the results. That way you'll get greater engagement from your team, which will make you achieve great results.

You will be successful in communicating with people when you are able to identify communication styles and when you are able to adapt as the situation demands. The most suitable thing is to bet on assertive communication and clearly convey the message to the different publics of the company.

Therefore, developing oratory techniques and improving verbal and non-verbal communication to use them in your favor are good alternatives. Below, we suggest some practical actions to reverse the negative effects of inefficient communication and thus better manage your teams, even from a distance.

1. Hold one-on-one meetings regularly

One-on-one meetings are advantageous because they allow time with the followers, even if virtually. Frequency and regularity make employees feel noticed and listened to.

In this way, the manager is able to resolve outstanding issues directly, even offering the support that the professional needs.

2. Hold general meetings

Individual meetings should not suppress meetings between all members of the organization. This can be done in the same online environment, in order to increase alignment, especially when the company experiences some instability. Take advantage of these occasions to celebrate achievements, present results, define next actions, listen to feedback from each department and also to connect and exchange ideas.

3. Develop shared workspaces online

On the internet, there are good tools for project management that can be used by teams. A strategy that manages to keep employees informed about projects and progress in each area, in addition to deadlines and difficulties.

4. Perform team building activities

Team building is a kind of training that, instead of proposing the technical improvement of employees, promotes the deepening of interpersonal relationships. Thus, activities such as book club, various tests, game night, challenges are welcome, however, in a virtual way.

These are opportunities in which team spirit is renewed and social relationships are strengthened.

Everyone has his/her own preferred way of communicating with other people. Understanding what yours is helps develop a healthy interpersonal interactivity and increased productivity in a sustainable workplace when you know what people want.

One of the most common ways is to observe how people communicate: do they use body language, tone of voice, gestures or even what they say and not how they say it? Learning about this can help us identify how best to communicate with others.

Here are some basic tips to help you adapt your work style so that communication flows easily:

1. If someone is saying one thing, but their body language and facial expression suggest otherwise, believe what you see before what you hear; it's not always easy to read people, especially when there is a difference in culture or experience. So, try not to be offended when they're communicating something different than how they look.

2. If a person remains evasive despite having been asked for an explanation directly, it may mean that he does not want to explain further or even understand his situation better because he may simply lack motivation or interest in doing so. In such a situation, you should be careful not to push too hard. It's very important to respect other people's boundaries and that includes non-verbal communication.

3. If someone is being rude or disrespectful, it may mean they're simply having a bad day or don't like you for whatever reason and that it has nothing to do with you personally - in this case, the best thing you can do sometimes, is simply ignore them and if necessary, speak with your boss about the situation.

It can be quite difficult to read body language of strangers as well as that of co-workers especially when we are not familiar with their culture.

4. When asking a question try not to do so in an interrogative tone, instead observe your body language and tone of voice while doing so because both can be misunderstood or interpreted differently than how you intended them to be: too much inflection doesn't help as well; neither does too little. Again, we end up sounding too arrogant or just plain boring. The amount of inflection needed depends largely on the subject and how it's being presented; a presentation about financial figures or report is best kept low-key whereas one related to art, for example, is worth making more expressive.

5. When presenting something try your best to keep your emotions out of the equation, be objective and professional in whatever you're saying otherwise it's not only ineffective but also counterproductive by upsetting other people who may be involved and that could cause a lot of trouble later on down the road. This does not mean you cannot bring up something controversial if required, just make sure you know where everyone stands before doing so.

6. Be mindful of the fact that each one of us is on a different level, hence the way you present your opinion could be acceptable to some and not so much to others; for example, when discussing something with an older or younger person avoid using slang. It's just better to be professional at all times because it keeps things less complicated.

This can make a big difference in how people perceive you; they may think you are seeking attention by trying too hard to sound cool and later may try ignoring what you have to say, even when it's important.

The most important thing though is that we treat others fairly and respectfully because how we communicate really does matter!

But for communication to be efficient and assertive, two points are fundamental: learning to listen and transmitting what needs to be said clearly and objectively. Therefore, it is important to know the existing communication styles and also the particularities of each employee.

CHAPTER FOUR

THE IMPORTANCE OF UNDERSTANDING COMMUNICATION STYLES

Understanding how people communicate with each other is vitally important for both managers and employees. It allows you to recognize specific needs or problems that an individual may have at work, reducing the amount of time needed to address them directly. This can only be achieved by paying close attention as you engage with business partners, customers, suppliers or even colleagues within your own company. Observing the body language of others (for example, looking to see if they are making direct eye contact) will help you gain insight into their mindsets while also enabling you to better tailor your own message.

Another way you can enhance this is through regular or scheduled meetings with your staff. This allows them to ask your advice, give feedback or request resources, without fear of reprimand or unfair treatment on their part and also helps you stay abreast in the loop for ongoing business operations.

Although understanding good interpersonal communication is essential for building strong relationships, it's difficult to achieve without some common ground. However even if there are cultural differences that prevent full comprehension from one party to another, a little effort can go a long way toward making the other person feel valued and respected by expressing genuine interest in what they have to say. It's important to remember that everyone has something different to offer; depending on how well you know someone, you could be surprised at the valuable insight they possess.

If you feel that someone may have difficulty communicating effectively, why not offer to sit down with them and go through some problem-solving techniques or tools together? Even if it's simply a matter of their speech being fast or quiet, there are ways in which this can be worked around to provide a better working environment for all involved.

Remember that by identifying others' strengths and weaknesses through communication styles, you're helping them feel more valued and respected as an individual rather than dismissing ideas based on miscommunication.

It's also important to be aware of your own communication style so that you can adapt your mannerisms and interactions accordingly. You must not dominate the conversation on every occasion or dump all the responsibility for a project on to one coworker, as these actions may hinder their ability to perform effectively.

Lastly, it is vital that you read between the lines when listening during meetings or in client communications. A face-to-face conversation reveals much more information than an email interaction and should not be taken lightly. Using context clues such as facial expressions will enable you to engage more meaningfully with those around you and encourage them to do the same with us too.

It is also worth bearing in mind that different people will have varying levels of tolerance those with strong communication skills are able to work with those having little or no skill of this kind.

Because of the challenges involved in these situations, it is important that you find ways to adapt your own communication style so that negative consequences can be avoided.

Communication styles as a source of conflict and solutions.

People have different preferences when it comes to communicating with others, which means they are likely to interpret messages differently from one another. In order for them not to miscommunicate, it's prudent for them to know their own and each other's preferred styles. This will help avoid costly misunderstandings by providing clarity beforehand about how things might transpire between them. In many cases, people don't even realize there is a better way of communicating with one another. They may think they are doing it right and the other party is to blame for any communication issues that arise later on.

Learning about each other's preferred styles will allow you to stop such issues from escalating!

Behavioral style theory explains why these differences occur. The four categories: Extroverted (E), introverted (I), sensing (S) and feeling (F), form a basis for understanding how individuals prefer to communicate with others, as well as process their thoughts and feelings. An extrovert gets his or her energy from interacting with others while an introvert derives it in quiet isolation. A sensor relies on tangible or practical things to make decisions while a feeler relies upon "gut instinct" or emotions.

If you're not aware of your own style or others' styles, miscommunication may ensue and this could lead to serious problems on the job or in a working relationship. This is why it's essential for all individuals involved to be aware of their preferred communication styles and those of other people if they are to develop positive relationships with everyone involved.

The most productive work environment relies upon an understanding between employees, managers and company owners that avoids conflict between them due to a lack of effective communication skills. If you are ever concerned about your ability (or someone else's) to maintain such a relationship, get assistance from experts in human resources or outside consultants who know how to solve problems related to interpersonal communications in the workplace.

All parties involved should make themselves more aware of the importance of improving their own communication skills as well as be willing to work with others so that any conflicts between them due to misunderstandings or lack of clarity can be overcome for the sake of a healthy and productive workplace environment.

CHAPTER FIVE

CONCLUSION

The importance of knowing and understanding how others communicate with us is difficult to stress enough. Especially since we spend up to a good third of our working lives communicating. It is also important to understand that different people have different communication styles, so when dealing with people who may not be used to your way of communicating, you need to make an effort in order for both parties to be at ease.

Remember that if the communication channels are blocked, the project can end up being delayed or even canceled which will certainly affect productivity on all levels.

Understanding different communication styles leads to better interpersonal interaction in the workplace (interpersonal skill), increased productivity for teams, and ultimately greater profitability for businesses in general.

However, communication is not limited to verbal and non-verbal. It's a combination of different styles that allows us to deliver messages effectively. In business, being able to work with others successfully is important otherwise it results in less productivity due to lack of employee satisfaction and low performing workers.

As company owners, managers will have to make sure their staff is able to communicate effectively within the business and in other industries and it can only be achieved if the manager understands the different communication styles. This makes it possible for the manager to be aware of what they do or say (i.e., their behavior) that may not be understood by others who have a different communication style.

Different co-workers with different thoughts and feelings, how they interpret information/feedback will affect interpersonal interactivity within the work place. This is something that should be considered by all managers for an effective working environment because if there are "negative" feedbacks from employees, low morale and low productivity will result in over years, affecting company performance negatively irrespectively of how much profit the business earns. This also means that managers should have the ability to adapt to different situations and be flexible in providing feedback to employees for a sustainable workplace relationship.

There are many factors influencing the way we communicate such as our wellbeing (we react differently when sick), sexuality (men and women do not express feelings in the same way), cultural background, education level (i.e., if they had an extensive education or they only received formal primary school education). Therefore, effective communication is vital for any business to thrive.

Another important aspect is for a manager to be flexible in understanding what the employees are trying to say when communicating with them because each employee has different communication styles. This will not only help their business but also make it easier for the staff to communicate with one another in the work place as well and reduce conflict of interest within the company.

www.ingramcontent.com/pod-product-compliance
Lightning Source LLC
Chambersburg PA
CBHW070136230526
45472CB00004B/1561